floral decorations for entertaining with style

• • •

terry l. rye

floral decorations for entertaining with style

● ● ●

terry l. rye

NORTH LIGHT BOOKS

www.artistsnetwork.com
cincinnati, ohio

about the author

Terry Rye's passion for flowers has allowed her the best job in the world—creating innovative and beautiful floral designs. Since 1980 she has been the owner of Mariemont Florist in Cincinnati, Ohio. Mariemont Florist has been featured in the prestigious Cincinnati Flower Show and is listed in the distinguished international directory *Fine Flowers by Phone*. As a self-taught floral designer, Rye loves to share the joy of floral arranging with others. She resides in Cincinnati, Ohio, with her seven-year-old daughter, Sarah.

dedication

I dedicate this book in memory of my grandparents, to my daughter,

Sarah, and to my loving family and friends for their support and

encouragement throughout my life.

Floral Decorations for Entertaining With Style. © 2002 by Terry L. Rye. Manufactured in China. All rights reserved. No part of this book may be reproduced in any form or by any electronic or mechanical means including information storage and retrieval systems without permission in writing from the publisher, except by a reviewer, who may quote brief passages in a review. Published by North light Books, an imprint of F&W Publications, Inc., 4700 East Galbraith Road, Cincinnati, Ohio 45236. (800) 289-0963. First edition.

Other fine North light Books are available from your local bookstore, or art supply store or direct from the publisher.

06 05 04 03 02   5 4 3 2 1

Library of Congress Cataloging-in-Publication Data

Rye, Terry L.,
    Floral decorations for entertaining with style/ by Terry L. Rye.
    p. cm.
Includes bibliographical references (p.).
ISBN 1-55870-598-8 (alk. paper)
1. Flower arrangement. 2. Floral decorations. I. Title.

SB449. R87 2002
647.92--dc21

                    2001056736

editors: Tricia Waddell and Karen Roberts
designer: Andrea Short
production coordinator: Sara Dumford
production artist: Rebecca Blowers
photo Stylists: Jan Nickum and Laura Robinson
photographers: Christine Polomsky and Al Parrish

acknowledgements

Many thanks to all the dedicated people in my business, Mariemont Florist, for their support and loyalty during the completion of this book and for their contributions. I am truly blessed with a talented staff, wonderful friends and an incredibly supportive, loving family.

Many thanks to my editor Tricia Waddell for her continued encouragement and enthusiasm. Her team of true professionals is dedicated to publishing the very best in floral craft books. I am proud to be a part of her team. Also, I want to thank Karen Roberts for her editorial expertise in helping create a book that is full of entertaining ideas, easy to understand and filled with fun projects. My warm appreciation to Christine Polomsky for the beautiful instructional photos in every project and her support and laughter throughout the photo shoot.

Through my passion for flowers and sharing it with others, my life has been enriched greatly. I am so grateful for the love of my family and friends and the opportunities that have come my way. Life is not a dress rehearsal but a wealth of relationships, experiences and achievements. Living life to its fullest and making a difference to others is important to me and remembered each day through my daughter, Sarah.

introduction • 9

entertaining with style • 10

basic tools and supplies • 14

selecting flowers • 16

• **dinner** parties

a night in the far east • 20

into the wild • 28

south seas paradise • 36

white elegance • 46

● ● ● ● ● ● ● ● ●

section one

Decorating your table with

beautiful flowers can

make your party **a feast for the**

eyes as well as **for the** body

and mind.

20

PAGE

• special occasions

bridesmaid tea party • 58

birthday surprise • 66

garden party • 76

romantic dinner for two • 84

• • • • • • • • • •

section two

• home for the holidays

mother's day brunch • 92

halloween party • 98

thanksgiving feast • 106

christmas at home • 116

• • • • • • • • • •

section three

66
PAGE

116
PAGE

resources • 125

index • 126

introduction

I have spent the past twenty years creating beautiful floral arrangements. Nothing makes me happier than to surround myself with beautiful flowers and creative people and share my passion for creating floral displays for all occasions. The goal of *Floral Decorations for Entertaining With Style* is to inspire you and spark your creativity when planning a gathering with friends and family. Creating an evening full of good conversation, great food and wonderful surroundings is the mark of a great host. The surroundings begin when you greet your guests at the door and continue with the atmosphere you create in the setting of your table. I have always felt that the difference between a great party and a truly memorable one is the length of time your guests remain seated, deep in conversation, as well as sharing friendship and delicious food. Decorating your table with beautiful flowers can make your party a feast for the eyes as well as for the body and mind.

Beautiful flowers invite guests to the table and make dining at home a **luxurious experience.**

Flowers are an easy way to turn an ordinary dining table into an extraordinary one. They simply add grandeur to an event as no other element can. A lush floral centerpiece surrounded by beautiful floral decorations at each setting can create a table that is dramatic yet intimate. Beautiful flowers invite guests to the table and make dining at home a luxurious experience.

The ideas and projects presented in this book are theme oriented for exceptional table decorations. Every project presented shows how you can use silk and dried flowers in imaginative ways to design a uniquely beautiful table. To create stylish table centerpieces and floral decorations all you need is a sense of adventure and a desire to have fun. Whether you are hosting a formal dinner or a casual afternoon brunch, this book will show you how you can use flowers to set a table with style and flair.

terry l. rye

entertaining with style

Whether your style is casual or formal, contemporary or traditional, setting a beautiful table is a great way to express your personality and creativity and make your guests feel welcome. Creating a beautiful table doesn't have to be a lot of work or cost a lot of money. There are millions of ways to decorate a table, and a little imagination and planning go a long way toward creating something stylish. The most important thing is to keep things manageable so that the planning is fun and you enjoy the meal.

••• creating a theme

Whether you're celebrating a family holiday, a special occasion or a dinner party with friends, decorating your table around a theme can turn an ordinary meal into a memorable event. Use your theme as your inspiration to create a specific mood or atmosphere for your next gathering. Carry your theme throughout the table, from the floral decorations and menu to your choice of table settings, tablecloth, napkins and place mats. This is a great way to make entertaining at home creative, personal and fun.

••• flowers for the table

Flowers are the focal point when it comes to creating uniquely beautiful table decorations. Choose flower colors that visually tie all the elements of your table together. Pay attention to the size of your table and the number of guests in order to design your table flowers so all your guests can see and interact with one another around your centerpiece.

Your choice of floral container also sets the tone for your table. Try a pitcher or basket for outdoor entertaining, or use decorative glasses, urns or pottery for an informal dinner party. Try using multiple vases to create an interesting effect. Cluster small containers, such as cordial glasses or small pitchers, to give the table a personal feeling. Or use hollowed-out fruits and vegetables for containers that are fun and full of color. You can even dress up a plain glass or clay container by covering it with large leaves, such as magnolia, oak, galax or bay, then add a pretty ribbon or trim as a finishing touch.

• thanksgiving feast:
Use the warm colors of autumn as your inspiration to create flowers for an elegant Thanksgiving table.

••• decorative details

Entertaining with style is all in the details. Adding simple, finishing touches to your table makes any gathering of friends and family more intimate and allows you to express your individual style. Flowers can be used throughout the table, not just in the centerpiece, to add colorful accents. Wrap a single flower stem around a napkin for a beautiful napkin ring. Place small containers of flowers or potted plants at each table setting for unique place card holders. Use a few blooms or greenery to decorate around the base of candles or serving platters. Sprinkle rose petals randomly around the table for a romantic touch. Use seasonal accents, such as acorns, gourds and small pumpkins for fall or pinecones and berries for winter, throughout the table or as a party favor at each guest's table setting. Even garnishing food with individual blooms of small, edible flowers dusted with sugar is a great way to enhance the presentation of the food and create a stunning table.

Another creative way to decorate your table is with ribbons. Choose ribbons that complement your flowers in color and texture as well as suit the occasion. For example, velvet or taffeta ribbons in deep colors are perfect for a winter holiday dinner, while grosgrain ribbons in soft colors are a romantic addition to a table set for a garden party or outdoor wedding. Tie coordinating ribbons around pillar candles for a finishing touch. Use ribbons in place of napkin rings, and tie on a short flower as an accent. Think beyond traditional ribbons, and use raffia or dried grasses for a more natural look. Dress up a vase or flowerpot with a soft bow for a casual garden look, or add drama to a buffet table by draping it with ribbon. Regardless of what style you choose for the occasion, there are endless possibilities for adding creative embellishments to your table.

••• table settings

The most exciting part of entertaining is taking what you already have and finding a creative way to use it. Most of us don't have dozens of different sets of dishes, silver-

• mother's day brunch: Choose a focal flower and a sprig of greenery from your arrangement to make a coordinated napkin ring.

• a night in the far east: An Asian-themed table featuring votive candle holders covered in dried grass and pebble place mats show how you can use texture to create unique table settings.

ware, glassware or table linens to choose from for every occasion. The trick is to dress up what you have to fit the occasion and coordinate it with your table flowers and decorations. Try learning a creative napkin folding technique. Drape a favorite shawl across a plain tablecloth for added drama, or use a long scarf as a table runner. Mix and match dishes, flatware and glassware for a casual dinner with friends. Rather than conforming to formal dining etiquette, experiment and let your own style be your guide in setting a beautiful table.

••• lighting

Good lighting adds ambiance to any occasion. It makes food look appetizing and flowers look spectacular, and it sets the mood for your guests. Use dimmed or indirect lighting for entertaining indoors, and nothing beats candlelight for setting a dramatic table at night, inside or out.

Candles come in all shapes, sizes and colors, but no matter what kind you choose, they add warmth and intimacy to any gathering. Select candle holders that coordinate with the table and protect your linens and flowers from wax and candle dyes. Use candles of various shades to accent your table, or use simple ivory candles when using colored candle holders so that the light shines through clearly and creates a soft effect. Use dripless candles in your floral centerpiece, or place candles of various heights throughout your table for a dramatic look.

Scented candles can add a soothing fragrance to a room but may be overpowering in a small area or compete with the aroma of food. Try mixing scented candles with unscented ones for a delicate scent, or use only unscented candles in your dining area.

••• creating a mood

Creating an intimate environment in which your guests feel relaxed, comfortable and welcome is the mark of a good host. The secret to this is good planning so you have plenty of time to prepare for your guests' arrival and you are not too busy in the kitchen or stressed with last-minute details to enjoy the evening yourself.

• **mood lighting:** Candles add a dramatic touch to any floral arrangement.

••• candle **tips & tricks** •••

Whether you are using votives, tapers, pillars, tea lights or floating candles on your table, here are a few helpful hints to follow:

• Trim candlewicks to approximately ½" (13mm) so the flame will not smoke. Make sure the wick is not too short, or the flame will drown in the molten wax and may cause the candle to drip excessively.

• When purchasing candles, pay attention to the burning time listed on the label. You do not want your candles to burn down before your party is over.

• Pay attention to the quality of the candle. An inexpensive candle may not have a long burning time. If the candle burns too quickly, it could be dangerous and catch your arrangements or table linens on fire or drip wax onto the table.

• Use a few drops of hot candle wax to secure tapers in their holders and keep the candles straight.

• Add a small amount of water to a votive candle holder before adding the candle. This makes it easy to clean out the melted wax. If you forget to do this ahead of time, run hot water over the bottom of the candle holder and the candle should slide right out.

• Here's an easy way to get melted wax out of table linens: Lay your linen flat and place a brown paper bag over the candle wax. Place a warm iron on the bag, and move slowly over the melted wax area. The bag will absorb the wax and remove it from the linen. Repeat if necessary.

Once you have planned the food and table decorations, there are a few easy ways to create a mood for a memorable occasion. Music can create a magical background throughout the entire meal. Make sure it's appropriate for the occasion and kept low enough so it doesn't overpower party conversation.

Light scents enhance the dining area. In addition to candles, there are wonderful room sprays and potpourris available to create a festive or holiday mood. For example, you can use pine scent for a winter get-together, rose for a romantic dinner or wedding, cinnamon at Christmas or pumpkin spice for Thanksgiving. Add a floral spray scent to your silk or dried arrangement for a delicate fragrance on the table. Just remember not to overdo it.

Make sure your guests have comfortable chairs for sitting at the dining table, with plenty of elbow and leg room. When space on the dining table is at a premium, serve the meal buffet style for more relaxed entertaining. Coordinate your table decorations with elements on your buffet table, mantel or chandelier or in any other room where people will eat.

⋯ entertaining outdoors

Whether you choose to entertain your guests in your garden or yard, at poolside or on the porch, or on your terrace or balcony, let the natural decorations supplied by Mother Nature be your guide. Flowers arranged in a loose, casual style look best for table decorations outside.

Silk and dried flowers fade when exposed to the sun for long periods of time. Protective floral sprays and sealants can keep your flowers looking bright. In addition, excessive humidity can spoil paper products, ribbons and bows, and dried flowers can become moist and spoil. Place these items in shady areas whenever possible.

Weight floral containers with sand or marbles to prevent centerpieces from being blown over by wind. Avoid using tall, slender vases or fragile arrangements outside. Protect candles from drafts with glass hurricanes or by setting short candles inside tall candle holders, and use citronella candles to deter insects. When entertaining at night, add strings of lights around the dining area so guests can see clearly. Then just sit back, relax and enjoy the fresh air.

• **south seas paradise:**
A deck surrounded by woodland trees provides a dramatic setting for entertaining outdoors.

basic tools and supplies

To create all the arrangements and floral decorations in this book, you need a few basic tools and supplies. All of these materials are inexpensive and available in the floral section of your local craft store.

1. chenille stem: Chenille stems are similar to pipe cleaners and are used in securing bows, anchoring floral foam and strengthening stems. They consist of bendable, twisted, heavy wire and a flocked material that allows water to flow through.

2. floral adhesive: Floral adhesive is a dependable glue for wet or dry surfaces. It does not require heating and dries clear. For best results, add it to a surface and let it sit until it is tacky before adhering it. If you cannot find floral adhesive in your local craft store, you can purchase it from your local florist. You can also use craft glue or Elmer's glue as a substitute.

3. floral anchor: Floral anchors are small plastic holders used to secure floral foam in the bottom of a container.

4. floral foam: Dry floral foam is used for dried and silk flowers. It is more dense and firm than wet foam. You can buy floral foam in a range of sizes and forms. I prefer the foam blocks for most centerpieces. You can easily cut the blocks to size with a kitchen knife or stack them to fit any container.

5. floral pick: Wooden floral picks come in several sizes and are useful in securing bows, extending stem lengths and anchoring candles into arrangements. These sticks come with or without wire attached.

6. floral scent: Available in various floral fragrances, floral-scented sprays are a wonderful way to add fragrance to a silk arrangement or floral craft project.

7. floral spray paint: Floral spray paints are wonderful for adding color to white foam or a topiary stem. You can use them for a range of floral craft projects.

8. floral tape: Use floral tape to secure flowers together or wrap stems or candles onto floral picks for easy insertion. This self-sealing tape is activated by the heat of your fingers and is available in shades of green, brown and white. Available in several widths, ¼" (6mm) wide floral tape was used in all projects.

9. greening pin: Sometimes called S-pins or floral pins, greening pins are metal pins used to secure moss or other floral materials to floral foam.

10. hot glue gun: You can use a hot glue gun for many floral craft projects. Use a glue gun with several heat settings. The lowest setting is hot enough to adhere materials safely. Do not use hot glue on floral foam because it will melt the foam.

11. paddle wire: Paddle wire is green floral wire that comes wrapped around a paddle for ease in holding with one hand to secure and wrap a group of stems, as in a garland.

12. plant stake: Plant stakes or hyacinth sticks are hard wooden stakes that give support to flowers with heavy heads or weak stems. They are available in various sizes and colors. Each plant stake has a pointed end for easy insertion into floral foam.

13. sealer: Use a spray sealer when working with dried materials to prevent shedding and breakage and to maintain the flowers' natural color.

14. wire cutter: You need wire cutters to cut silk flowers with thin stems or dried material. Heavier stems may require a stronger pair.

selecting flowers

••• silk flowers

There are so many varieties of artificial flowers available on the market. While the majority of artificial flowers are silk, you can also find flowers and foliages made of latex, paper and plastic. How can you choose which flowers are best for your arrangement? The quality of silk flowers can be seen in the colors, textures and details in the flower and foliage.

Quality silk flowers should be attached securely to the stem, and each stem should include numerous flowers. Choose flowers with colors that are true to their natural counterparts. Look for flowers with wired stems, petals and leaves so you can bend and mold each flower individually. If the stem will be hidden in floral foam in your arrangement, the quality of the stem is less important. Some of the high-quality silk flowers have very thick stems that can be hard to cut and separate. Make sure you have a strong pair of wire cutters when working with these stems.

In addition to buying flowers as single stems, you can also use flower picks in your arrangements. Picks have multiple flower varieties and foliage all on one stem. They are primarily used as accent or filler flowers or for very small, tight arrangements. They are an inexpensive alternative to buying individual stems. Generally, picks have short stems and are not a good choice for full designs or line arrangements.

••• opening silk flowers •••

Silk flowers are generally packaged very tightly with the flowers and foliage folded and flattened. Here's how to bring them to life.

1 open package
Most silk flower stems are folded up like this lily stem when you first buy them.

2 unfold flower
Begin unfolding the flower from the bottom. Start with the leaves and work your way up the stem. When opening the flowers, arrange the petals as naturally as you can.

3 mold the flower
Your silk flower takes on a fresh look when unfolded and molded by your hands. To keep your silk flowers and foliage looking fresh and free of dust, periodically wipe them off with a damp cloth or gently blow-dry the dust off the surface.

••• dried flowers and plants

When selecting dried flowers and foliage, choose materials that are not faded or shattered. Handle dried flowers with care since they are very fragile, and spray dried arrangements with a sealant to reduce shattering and decay. You can also use a light coat of dried flower sealant on ribbons and bows to protect and strengthen them against moisture and humidity.

Dried flowers and plants are available in craft stores, or you can dry flowers yourself from your own garden. Flowers can be air-dried, dried in silica gel or preserved through freeze-drying. Each process yields a slightly different result.

air-drying

While there are several methods of air-drying flowers, hanging them upside down in a dark, dry and well-ventilated place dries most varieties. When dry, the flowers will be smaller than their original sizes, color may be lost and the petals and leaves will have a wrinkled appearance. Most flowers dry within five days to two weeks.

silica gel

Available in most craft stores, silica gel is a powder that dries flower heads to a nearly fresh appearance within several days. It absorbs moisture from the flowers while supporting their natural shapes. You can reuse silica gel several times. Simply place the flower heads face up in a container partially filled with the silica gel powder, preferably an airtight container that is shallow and large in diameter. Gently sprinkle silica gel between the flower petals, then cover the flowers completely with the powder. Tightly cover the container with a lid, and allow the flowers to dry for two to seven days. Check the progress daily so the flowers do not overdry and become brittle. Finally, remove the dried flowers with a slotted spoon, gently lifting them from the powder. Remove the excess silica gel from the flower petals with a soft brush. These flowers are now ready for arranging, but they need wire stems added for support.

freeze-drying

Freeze-drying is a relatively new and advanced drying process that can preserve a flower almost indefinitely. Freeze-dried flowers keep their shapes and colors, and are easy to use in arrangements. Their stems never have to be cut from the flower heads. The freeze-drier machine removes the water from the flower at subzero temperatures through a vacuum. The moisture is collected in a condensation chamber which is defrosted throughout the preservation time. The flowers are then warmed to room temperature. The whole process takes ten to fifteen days. This slow process allows the flowers to hold their natural sizes and shapes, as well as their vibrant colors. You can purchase freeze-dried flowers from craft stores or directly from a florist.

• **halloween party:**
Dried and preserved autumn leaves were used to create colorful place mats, perfect for a Halloween or fall gathering.

(LEFT) • white elegance: Lush blooms in shades of white set the tone for a table designed for a sophisticated dinner party.

(CENTER) • a night in the far east: Create an elegant Asian-inspired table by using a bold mix of dramatic flowers and natural materials and textures.

(RIGHT) • into the wild: The deep colors of Africa inspired this exotic centerpiece and coordinated placemat.

dinner parties

A theme dinner party is a great way to bring a group of friends together and an opportunity for you to express your personality and creativity. Set the mood for the evening in advance by sending an inspired invitation to match your theme.

a night in the far east
page 20

into the wild
page 28

south seas paradise
page 36

white elegance
page 46

Use your imagination to convey the spirit of the party, for example, if you're planning a South Seas theme, put a message in a bottle that includes the necessary information and hand deliver it. Or write the party details on a postcard that depicts an inviting beach or island. For an Asian-inspired dinner party, attach the invitation to a set of chopsticks. Or, rubber-stamp Chinese calligraphy on handmade paper for a simple but striking look. Handwritten invitations are the most personal, and you can find a wide range of handmade and decorative papers in craft stores for creating elegant and easy invitations. Above all, have fun coming up with ideas to get your guests in the spririt of the party. Don't forget to make make sure your invitation has all of the essential information: date and time, location and directions, type of celebration, RSVP date and contact information. If you want guests to dress for the theme, mention it in the invitation.

a night in the far east

● **Invite your friends to the Orient** for a memorable dinner full of good food and conversation. Create an Asian-inspired table set with exotic garden pebble place mats and a striking ikebana centerpiece featuring magnolias and flowering branches. Votive candle holders surrounded by iris grass and tied with raffia provide shimmering candlelight for an intimate atmosphere. Serve jasmine rice, stir-fry and sushi with tea, oriental-style beer or sake. Use chopsticks and authentic dinnerware, such as rice bowls or a tea set, to set the scene. Decorate with items designed with Zen simplicity or brightly colored silk lanterns to bring the magical and tranquil Far East into your home.

PROJECTS

1.
magnolia centerpiece
page 22

2.
iris grass votive
page 25

3.
pebble place mat
page 26

1. magnolia centerpiece

- flowering orchid branch with multiple stems
- 2 large magnolia stems with 3 large flowers, a bud and green leaves on each
- 15" (38cm) diameter black round plastic dish
- exotic garden pebbles
- green or sphagnum moss
- 2½" × 3½" (6cm × 9cm) dry floral foam
- floral anchor
- floral adhesive or hot glue gun

2. iris grass votive candle holder

- glass votive candle holder with straight sides
- votive candle

- natural raffia
- iris grass
- 3½" × ¼" (9cm × 6mm) rubber band

3. pebble place mat

- 12" × 18" (30cm × 46cm) cardboard
- exotic garden pebbles
- 60" (2m) black cording
- black matte spray paint
- 12" × 18" (30 cm × 45 cm) mesh batting
- floral adhesive or hot glue gun
- 1" to 2" (25mm to 51cm) brush

project 1. # **magnolia** centerpiece

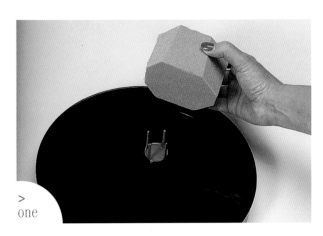

> one

> two

> three

1 prepare floral foam

Using floral adhesive or a hot glue gun, glue the floral anchor off center onto the dish. Cut a piece of dry floral foam 2½" x 3½" (6cm x 9cm), and trim the corners. Place the floral foam on the anchor lengthwise.

2 add moss

Apply floral adhesive or hot glue to the floral foam sparingly, and add the moss. Cover and shape the moss to the foam.

3 add exotic garden pebbles

Pour the pebbles into the dish approximately ¾" (19mm) thick, covering the bottom.

> five

> four

> six

4 add magnolia

Cut three small separate stems of magnolia to 5", 7" and 15" (13cm, 18cm and 38cm). Insert the 5" (13cm) stem into the side of the foam, placing it low over the pebble area. Insert the 15" (38cm) stem into the center top and back of the centerpiece, and place the 7" (18cm) low in between the two other stems. Remember to open and mold each flower petal.

5 add last magnolia

Cut a 4½" (11cm) magnolia stem. Curve the stem and insert it into the back of the foam. Cut and insert a bud near the magnolia stem.

6 insert leaves

Cut a few remaining leaves from the magnolia stem and insert them randomly into the foam. Make sure leaves are placed close to the stems that have already been inserted for a natural appearance.

··· helpful **hint** ···

Create a flowing and uneven line with the magnolia stems to achieve a natural look. Bend the flowers up slightly to give the appearance that they are growing toward the sun.

7 add flowering orchid stem

Cut an 18" (46cm) orchid stem, and insert it behind the center of the tallest magnolia.

8 insert remaining stems

Cut approximately five more stems in varying lengths from 5" to 10" (13cm to 25cm). Randomly insert them near the magnolia stems.

> seven

> eight

Designer Tip

To create a variation on this centerpiece, substitute the magnolias with camellias, peonies or fuji mums.

iris grass votive candle holder

> one

1 cut iris grass

Measure the iris grass against the votive candle holder, and cut to your desired length.

2 cover the votive

Wrap the rubber band around the votive candle holder twice. Slide the iris grass under the rubber band. Insert a letter opener or dull knife under the rubber band to make it easier to insert the grass.

> two

> three

3 trim the iris grass

Insert the iris grass completely around the votive holder, and trim at staggering lengths. Wrap raffia around the votive holder, and then tie it in a square knot to hold.

Designer Tip

Pour a little water in the votive candle holder to prevent the candle wax from adhering to the glass. For added color, insert a silk flower under the raffia.

pebble place mat

> one

> two

1 prepare the cardboard

Spray paint matte black on the 12" x 18" (30cm x 45cm) cardboard. Allow it to dry in a ventilated area. Round the corners of the cardboard.

2 prepare the batting

Spray paint matte black on the 12" x 18" (30cm x 45 cm) batting. Allow it to dry in a ventilated area. Round the corners of the batting.

> three

3 adhere batting to cardboard

Glue the batting to the cardboard with floral adhesive or a hot glue gun.

> four

> five

4 apply the pebbles

Use a wide brush to spread a thick coat of floral adhesive or hot glue. Cover and press the garden pebbles into the glue.

5 add cording

Glue 60" (2m) of black cording and around the perimeter of the place mat.

Designer Tip

Use additional place mats under hot serving dishes, the centerpiece or the candles to create a more dramatic table.

into the wild

● **Spice up your next dinner party** with a table inspired by an African safari. Create a centerpiece using animal print fabric and burlap wrapped around a clay pot filled with exotic dried and silk flowers. Complete the table with place mats of frosted galax leaves for a table set with unique style. Add candles all around to fill the air with a light scent of ethnic spices. Prepare a menu with cuisine from Morocco to Kenya, use inexpensive global handicrafts as unique party favors for your guests and let music set the tone for a night filled with exotic surprises.

PROJECTS

1.
safari centerpiece
page 30

2.
galax leaf place mat
page 35

1. safari centerpiece

- 1 bunch of protea
- 1 bunch of purple amaranthus
- 1 bunch of yellow amaranthus
- 4 to 5 thistle stems
- 8" (20cm) diameter clay pot
- sphagnum moss
- 12" (30 cm) square taper candle
- 1 yard (1m) of burlap
- 1 yard (1m) of two-sided animal print fabric
- 1 brick of dry floral foam
- floral anchor
- 12" (32cm) hyacinth stick (PLANT STAKE)

- green waterproof floral tape
- greening pins
- large rubber band
- hot glue gun

2. galax leaf place mat

- large frosted galax leaf bush
- 12" × 18" (30cm × 46cm) cardboard
- black matte spray paint
- hot glue gun

project 1. # safari centerpiece

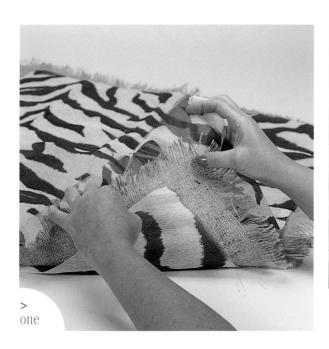

>
one

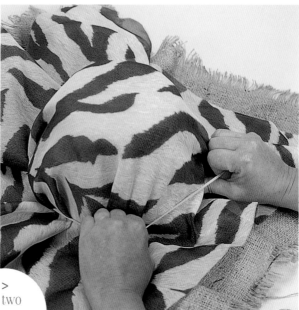
>
two

1 cut burlap and animal fabric

Cut two pieces of animal fabric to 28" x 25" (71cm x 64cm). Cut the burlap to 30" x 32" (76cm x 81cm). Fray the ends of the burlap on all four sides. Place the burlap in between the two layers of animal fabric.

2 cover the clay pot

Place the three pieces of fabric over the inverted clay pot, and secure the fabric to the pot with a rubber band. Pull the rubber band toward the rim of the pot.

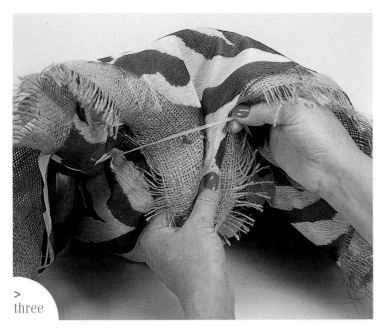

> three

3 tuck the fabric corners

Take all four corners of the fabric
and tuck the ends underneath the
rubber band. Allow the fabric to
hang over the rubber band.

> four

> five

4 add the floral anchor

Hot glue the floral anchor into the bottom of the pot.

5 insert the dry floral foam

Insert a block of dry floral foam into the pot on the floral anchor.

··· helpful **hint** ···

When using a 6" (15cm) clay pot, the animal fabric should measure 20" × 20"
(51cm × 51cm) and the burlap should measure 26" × 24" (66cm × 61cm).

>
six

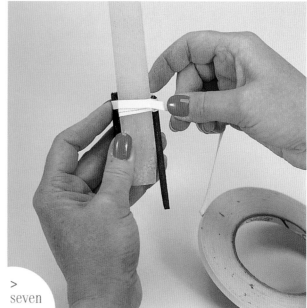

>
seven

6 trim the floral foam

Trim the floral foam so it is even with the rim of the pot. Cut the extra foam into two pieces, and wedge them into the sides of the pot for more stability.

7 prepare candle

Cut the hyacinth stick into four 3" (8cm) pieces. Trim the ends of the sticks at an angle for easier insertion. Use waterproof floral tape to attach the sticks to each side of the candle. Tape one stick at a time. Allow the ends of the sticks to extend 1" (3cm) below the end of the candle. Wrap the tape around the candle and the sticks to secure.

8 insert the candle

Insert the candle in the middle of the foam.

>
eight

9 cover with moss

Cover the foam with dampened sphagnum moss, and secure with a few greening pins.

10 add protea

Cut the protea to 2" (5cm) stems from the base of the flower. Randomly insert them into the foam at various angles.

11 add thistle

Cut approximately eight thistle sprigs with 2" (5cm) stems, and cut at least four sprigs with 5" (13cm) stems. Insert these stems throughout the centerpiece. Add more if desired.

> nine

> ten

> eleven

••• helpful **hint** •••

Add more moss if the tape at the base of the candle is still exposed.

> twelve

12 add amaranthus

Cut sprigs from both the purple and yellow amaranthus at various heights with stems from 2" to 5"(5cm x 13cm). Insert the stems throughout the centerpiece, placing the longer trailing stems on the sides and the shorter trailers in the center. It is helpful to insert one color of amaranthus at a time. Bend the stems that are in the way of the candle. Insert the extra foliage.

> thirteen

13 adjust rubber band

Pull the rubber band up and over the rim of the pot, and fluff out the fabric.

• • • • • • • • • •

Designer Tip

Create more centerpieces using the same method, but vary the sizes of the pots and the variety of animal print fabric, for example, tiger or snakeskin. Create a variation of this centerpiece with a 10" (25cm) pot to add drama to a buffet table.

galax leaf place mat

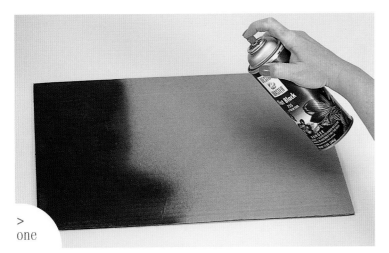

> one

1 prepare cardboard

Spray the piece of 12" x 18" (30cm x 46cm) cardboard with black matte spray paint. Allow it to dry in a ventilated area.

2 cover the cardboard place mat

Cut off the frosted galax leaves from the bush, and hot glue them onto the cardboard. Let the leaves extend past the edges of the cardboard, and completely cover the cardboard with overlapping leaves.

> two

Designer Tip

Cut any leftover galax leaves from the stems. Wrap each galax leaf around a napkin and staple the ends together to create a coordinated napkin ring.

south seas paradise

● **Create a romantic evening in the South Seas** by transforming your home into a tropical paradise. Pair a beautiful and dramatic centerpiece of orchids, river cane and ornamental grasses with a shimmering array of candles atop coordinating candle trivets. Surround the dining area with palm and other large potted plants. Greet your guests at the door with flower leis and fruity drinks (with or without the little umbrellas). Add tiki torches for entertaining outdoors, and serve grilled seafood, steamed rice and tropical fruit for a dinner inspired by the islands.

PROJECTS

1.
orchid centerpiece
page 38

2.
river cane candle trivet
page 45

1. orchid centerpiece

- 2 phalaenopsis orchid stems
- 3 vanda orchid stems
- 3 oncidium orchid stems
- 2 to 3 corkscrew willow stems
- 1 galax leaf bush
- 20' to 25' (6m to 8m) river cane
- 1 bunch of dried grass, 71" (2m) or longer
- 12" × 12" (30cm × 30cm) chicken wire
- dry floral foam brick
- green waterproof floral tape
- floral adhesive or hot glue gun
- 3½" × ¼" (9cm × 6mm) rubber band

2. river cane candle trivet

- 4' to 8' (1m to 2m) river cane
- 6" × 6" (15cm × 15cm) cardboard
- black matte spray paint
- floral adhesive or hot glue gun
- 4" (10cm) pillar candle (OPTIONAL)
- 48" (120cm) ornamental grass or raffia (OPTIONAL)

project 1. **orchid** centerpiece

1 cut river cane

Cut the river cane in varying heights from 14" to 25" (36cm to 64cm). Place the 14" (36cm) piece in the center of the others. Wrap the river cane twice with a rubber band.

2 arrange river cane

With the rubber band placed in the lower middle part of the river cane, rotate and spread out the river cane making sure the 14" (36cm) stem remains in the middle. This stem anchors the floral foam in the center of the arrangement. If a stem of river cane splits or breaks, add a dab of floral adhesive to repair it.

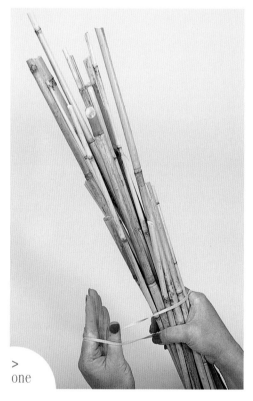

> one

> two

··· helpful **hint** ···

Arrange the centerpiece on a lazy Susan for improved accessibility to all sides to achieve a more balanced look.

> three

> four

3 trim floral foam and chicken wire

Cut floral foam to approximately 3" x 3" (8cm x 8cm). Wrap a
12" x 12" (30cm x 30cm) piece of chicken wire around the foam.

4 wrap floral foam with chicken wire

Fold the chicken wire completely around the foam, and trim
if necessary.

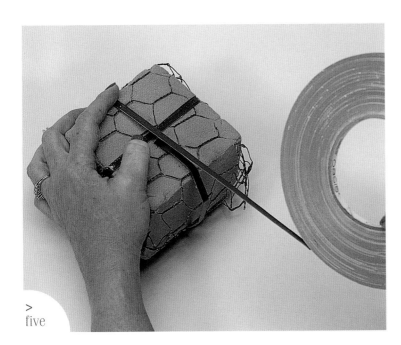

> five

5 secure the chicken wire

Wrap the floral tape around both the length and width of the foam and
chicken wire twice.

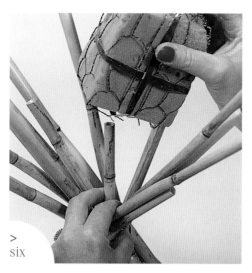

>
six

6 place the floral foam

Insert the 14" (36cm) river cane stem in the center of the floral foam. Keep this stem in the middle of the centerpiece.

7 create a balanced centerpiece

Spread out the river cane stems to shape and balance the centerpiece. Don't be concerned about the shape of the stems changing when creating the base of the centerpiece because the stems can always be adjusted throughout the arranging process.

8 cover the floral foam base with galax leaves

Cut individual 2" (5cm) stems of leaf clusters from the galax bush. Randomly insert the stems into the floral foam until the leaves cover the foam.

>
seven

>
eight

>
nine

>
ten

9   place the first phalaenopsis orchid stem

Cut one 20" (51cm) phalaenopsis orchid stem, and insert it into the top center of the foam. Bend the stem to trail over the left side of the centerpiece.

10   position the second phalaenopsis orchid stem

Insert another phalaenopsis orchid stem, 16" (41cm) long including a 3" (8cm) stem, in the top center of the foam, and bend the stem to the right. Placing thick stems near the center of the foam keeps the weight equally distributed and balances the centerpiece. Use floral adhesive or a hot glue gun to fill in holes when a stem is reinserted into the floral foam in a different spot.

11   add vanda orchid stems

Cut the three vanda orchid stems in varying lengths from 16" to 18" (41cm to 46cm), including a 2" (5cm) clean stem on each for insertion. To give the arrangement a more natural look, bend the stems to show a slight curve. Insert the stems into three separate sides of the floral foam.

>
eleven

••• helpful **hint** •••

When adding flowers to the centerpiece, always hold onto the center 14" (36cm) river cane stem to ensure stability.

> twelve

> thirteen

12 insert first oncidium orchid stem

Cut one stem of an oncidium orchid 27" (69cm) long with a 3" (8cm) stem. Insert it into the top center of the floral foam.

13 arrange final oncidium stems

Cut the two remaining oncidium orchid stems into two different lengths from 8" to 12" (20cm to 30cm). Add the final oncidium orchid stems in the lower sides of the floral foam and bend downward.

> fourteen

14 insert tall stem of corkscrew willow

Into the top of the centerpiece, add one 25" (64cm) branch of corkscrew willow that has two branches coming off of it. Substitute a lightweight flowering branch for the corkscrew willow if desired.

>
fifteen

>
sixteen

15 add remaining stems

Add remaining stems of corkscrew willow randomly throughout the arrangement.

16 braid the grass

Cut a section of grass approximately 71" (2m) long. Braid the grass and knot the ends.

17 tie the grass

Wrap the braided grass around the rubber band at the base of the centerpiece twice, and tie in a knot to finish.

>
seventeen

river cane candle trivet

> one

1 cut cardboard and paint

Spray a 6" x 6" (15cm x 15cm) piece of cardboard with black matte spray paint. Set it aside to dry. Whatever size pillar candle you use, add 1" (3cm) in each direction on the cardboard for the perfect size trivet.

> two

2 cut and glue river cane

Cut river cane in 6½" (17cm) stalks, enough to cover the cardboard. Using floral adhesive or hot glue, attach the river cane to the cardboard. Be sure the river cane lays flat and tight next to each other.

Designer Tip

For a 4" (10cm) pillar candle, cut a section of grass to 48" (1m) long. Knot each end, and wrap the grass twice around the candle. Finish with a double knot, and trim the excess grass to the desired length. Using two or more small candles on one trivet is very effective as well. For added interest, cut individual orchids from the stem and use them to enhance the table. Place the orchid blooms on each plate or at the base of the candle trivets. Create larger trivets for use under hot serving dishes.

white elegance

● **Enjoy an elegant evening by candlelight** and delicate blooms in subtle shades of white. Create a romantic centerpiece brimming over with open roses and poppies, surrounded by taper candles atop shimmering gold candlesticks embellished with ivy and delphinium. The best part of these floral decorations is that they are sophisticated yet easy to create. Harmonize the table decorations with beautiful table linens, china and a scattering of loose flowers all around. Make a splendid dinner party an intimate and comfortable occasion by following your own rules and setting your own style.

PROJECTS

1.
rose centerpiece
page 48

2.
floral candlesticks
page 52

1. rose centerpiece

- 1 bunch of dried amaranthus
- 2 open-rose stems
- 3 poppy stems
- 2 to 3 lisianthus stems
- 3 to 4 delphinium stems
- 2 frosted English ivy bushes
- 12" (30cm) pillar candlestick
- floral cage to fit candlestick
- floral lock

2. floral candlesticks

- 6 to 8 delphinium stems
- 2 frosted English ivy bushes
- pair of 8" to 10" (20cm to 25cm) glass candlesticks
- 2 dripless 12" (30cm) taper candles
- 2 candle adapters
- 6 floral picks (4" [10cm] each)
- dry floral foam brick
- green waterproof floral tape
- gold spray paint
- floral adhesive or hot glue gun

project 1. # rose centerpiece

> one

> two

2 insert roses

Cut roses to 3½" (9cm) stems. Insert the roses off center and on opposite sides of the centerpiece. This is a tightly arranged centerpiece. Be sure to insert fully. If any of the stems seem too loose and prone to falling out of the cage, secure them with floral lock.

1 insert floral cage

Insert the floral cage into the top of the candlestick.

> three

> four

> five

3 insert poppies

Insert one poppy with a 3" (8cm) stem in the top and center of the cage and two poppies with a 2" (5cm) stem on either side of the center. Remove some of the leaves on the stems.

4 add thin-stemmed amaranthus

Randomly add dried amaranthus with varying heights of 8" to 10" (20cm to 25cm). The stems can be fragile, so handle them with care. Insert the stems under the frame of the cage, and let the amaranthus hang over. Later a silk flower added under these delicate stems will take the weight off of the amaranthus.

5 add thick-stemmed amaranthus

Randomly add thick-stemmed amaranthus directly into the foam throughout the arrangement to desired fullness. If the amaranthus appears too long, trim to desired length.

> six

6 add lisianthus

Randomly insert lisianthus blooms with 2" (5cm) stems into the arrangement. Fill in the open spaces with larger blooms.

> seven

7 add lisianthus buds

Cut lisianthus buds to 2" (5cm) stems, and randomly insert them into the arrangement.

> eight

8 add delphinium

Cut a stem of delphinium into flower clusters with stems from 1" to 2" (3cm to 5cm) long. Randomly insert flower clusters throughout the centerpiece. Approximately three to four stems of delphinium are needed to fill in.

> nine

9 add frosted English ivy

Cut three ivy tips approximately 6" to 8" (15cm to 20cm) long, and insert them into the base of the cage and around the perimeter. Shape the ivy for a more natural look.

● ● ● ● ● ● ● ● ● ●

Designer Tip

*Fill in the arrangement with more
ivy of various lengths for
added fullness.*

floral candlesticks

> one

1 paint the candlesticks

Spray two candlesticks with gold spray paint.
When spraying, hold the can approximately 10"
(25cm) away from the candlestick. Don't forget to
paint the bottom of the candlestick. Allow to dry.

2 add candle adapters

Place the candle adapters into the tops of the
candlesticks securely. The rubber bottoms fit
snugly into the candlesticks.

> two

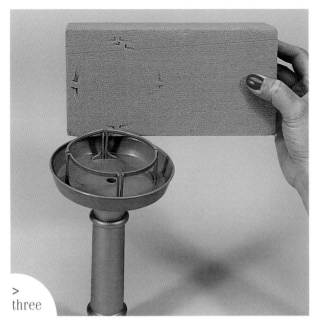

> three

> four

3 prepare dry floral foam

Press the floral foam on the top ring of a candle adapter to determine the size of the circles to be cut out and inserted into the holders. Cut out the foam circles and trim off one-third of the tops of the foam.

4 insert the foam

Glue the foam in the adapters with floral adhesive or a hot glue gun. Let the glue become tacky before securing the foam into the adapters.

> five

5 prepare candle holders

Cut six 4" (10cm) floral picks to 3" (8cm). With 1" (3cm) of the picks extending below the candle ends, begin taping three floral picks onto the base of each candle with waterproof floral tape. Tape one pick at a time. For greater stability, wrap the tape all the way up the length of the picks.

>
six

>
seven

6 insert candles

Push the candles into the centers of the foam, and adjust to make sure the candles are straight. Be sure your candles are dripless. Trim the wicks of the candles for a cleaner burning candle.

7 add delphinium

Using three to four stems of delphinium per candlestick, snip off sprigs of delphinium to approximately 4" to 5" (10cm to 13cm) long. Insert the sprigs into the foam and cover all around. Be sure to add enough sprigs near the bases of the candles to cover the floral picks.

8 add English ivy

Cut off various lengths of trailing sprigs of ivy from the bush. Insert the longest trailing stems around the candle bases, and insert others throughout the foam to fill in to desired fullness.

>
eight

• • • • • • • • • •

Designer Tip

*For a different look, remove the
arrangements and insert them
into new candlesticks.*

(LEFT) • **bridesmaid tea party:**
Make your bridesmaids' thank-you gifts more
special by creating rose potpourri gift boxes
and placing them at each tablesetting.

(CENTER) • **garden party:** Create topiary
place card holders that can also be used as
favors for your guests to take home as
mementos of the occasion.

(RIGHT) • **birthday surprise:** Find a
special something for each guest to fill these
colorful, whimsical party favor bags.

special occasions

Birthdays, weddings and other special occasions offer a great reason to entertain and get together with friends. To make any occasion a memorable event, always remember that comfort is the key, both for the guests and the hosts.

bridesmaid tea party
page 58

· ·

birthday surprise
page 66

· ·

garden party
page 76

· ·

romantic dinner for two
page 84

Consider finding someone to help before and during the party, so you won't be stuck in the kitchen preparing food. To be sure you have as much time with your guests as possible, prepare everything you can ahead of time—from the main course to the butter dish. Make appetizers bite-sized so guests can easily eat while mingling with drinks. Abundance is one sign of a good host, so be sure to have plenty of each dish for everyone. If necessary, rearrange furniture into several groupings of chairs so guests can easily talk with each other. One way to coordinate your color scheme is to line serving trays with linens that match, and place the trays on small tables near seating areas for easy reach. The most important tip: relax and enjoy the party! ●

bridesmaid tea party

● **Celebrate an upcoming wedding** with an elegant afternoon tea party for the bridesmaids. Typically held in the last two weeks before the wedding, it's a special opportunity for the bride to spend time with her bridal party before the wedding. Create a romantic table with a garden-inspired topiary filled with magnolias, roses and ivy wrapped with silk ribbon. Decorate small boxes with potpourri and silk ribbon roses to create delicately scented floral keepsake favor boxes. Inside each keepsake box, place a personal gift for each of the bridesmaids, such as a piece of jewelry to wear for the wedding.

PROJECTS

1.
sweetheart rose topiary
page 60

2.
potpourri favor box
page 64

1. sweetheart rose topiary

- 4 to 5 cosmos stems
- 8 to 10 sweetheart rose spray stems
- 5 to 7 frosted wild berry stems
- 4 to 6 magnolia sprays, 3 flowers per stem
- 3 variegated ivy bushes
- dark green ivy bush
- 3 to 6 yards (3m to 5m) ribbon rose garland
- 6" (15cm) diameter classic garden urn
- 5" (13cm) diameter topiary form
- greening pins
- forest green acrylic paint
- hot glue gun
- paper towels

2. potpourri favor box

- rose potpourri
- ribbon rose
- favor box
- ⅝" (16mm) moss green sheer chiffon ribbon, 30" (76cm) or longer
- rose scent spray
- hot glue gun

project 1. sweetheart rose topiary

1 paint topiary stem

Put a small amount of the forest green acrylic paint on a paper towel, and rub the paint onto the topiary stem to completely cover it.

> one

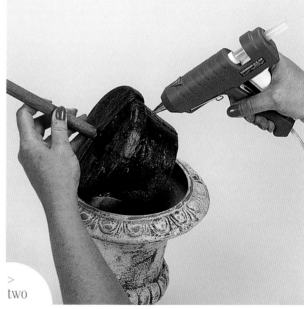

> two

2 secure topiary form

Apply hot glue to the base of the topiary form, and insert it into the urn to secure. Hold the glue gun away from the foam when applying the glue because the foam can melt.

> three

> four

3 add magnolia flowers

Cut magnolia flowers with 1" (3cm) stems. Insert them tightly around the topiary ball.

4 insert cosmos

Trim the cosmos to 1" to 2" (3cm to 5cm) stems. Insert the flowers and buds throughout the topiary ball. Insert the larger flowers first.

> five

> six

5 insert sweetheart spray roses

Cut the rose stems to 1" (3cm) below the first set of rose leaves from the base of the rose head. Insert the spray roses randomly around the ball at varying lengths. These roses extend out past the larger flowers. Add as many as desired.

6 add frosted wild berries

Cut the berry stems into 4" (10cm) sprigs, and insert them all around the topiary ball.

••• helpful **hint** •••

Do not take out flowers after inserting them. They will not remain secure if reinserted.

> seven

> eight

7 insert variegated and dark green ivy

Cut the desired amount of both types of ivy into 4" (10cm) sprigs, and completely fill in the topiary ball. Cut a few sprigs to 6" to 8" (15cm to20 cm), and insert them at the base of the topiary ball and around the top of the trunk. Use greening pins to help with insertion.

8 cover the topiary trunk

Cut a sprig of dark green ivy to approximately 17" (43cm). Insert the ivy into the bottom of the topiary ball, and secure with a greening pin. Wrap the ivy around and down the trunk. Secure it at the base of the trunk with greening pins. Make sure that some of the trunk is showing so it is more natural looking. Snip off a few leaves if necessary.

> nine

> ten

9 cover the topiary base

Cut various lengths of dark green ivy to 4" to 9" (10cm to 23cm), and insert them into the base of the topiary foam. Allow the ivy sprigs to trail down over the urn. Cover the base completely.

10 add variegated ivy

Insert a few sprigs of variegated ivy into the topiary base as desired.

> eleven

11 add ribbon rose garland

Start at the top of the topiary ball, and secure
one end of the garland at the top with a
greening pin. Begin wrapping and tucking the
garland with greening pins around the ball.
Completely cover the ball as desired using at
least 3 yards (3m) of garland.

• • • • • • • • • •

Designer Tip

*As a variation, double-wrap the ribbon
rose garland around the topiary and
insert a few flowers into the base.*

potpourri favor box

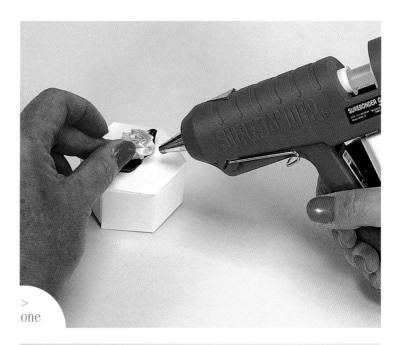

1   add the ribbon rose

Hot glue a ribbon rose to the center of the lid of a
plain white favor box.

2   cover the favor box

Cover the favor box with rose potpourri by hot
gluing the potpourri to the sides and top of the
box.

••• helpful **hint** •••

After unfolding and opening the favor box, put a piece of tape at the bottom
of the box to hold the fold.

> three

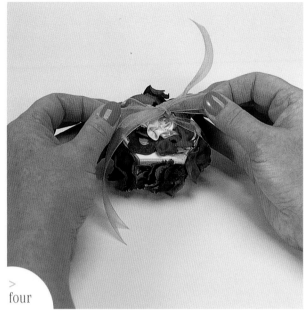

> four

3 add rose scent

Spray the box with the rose scent.

4 wrap the favor box

Insert the gift in the box. Cut the sheer chiffon ribbon to 30" (76cm), and wrap the ribbon around the box. Tie a square knot to close the box, and tie a bow.

● ● ● ● ● ● ● ● ● ●

Designer Tip

Trim the ribbon to the desired length. Different types of ribbon or potpourri could be substituted to achieve different looks.

birthday surprise

● **Celebrate your child's birthday** with a whimsical centerpiece featuring brightly colored flowers, candy garlands and lollipop flowers. Create party favor bags filled to the brim with sweet treats, trinkets and toys to delight your young guests. Add birthday cake, entertainment and games, and you've got a party your child will never forget!

PROJECTS

1.
birthday tree
page 68

2.
birthday favor bag
page 75

materials:

1. birthday tree

- 2 to 3 tree branches, 30" to 36" (76cm to 90cm)
- 3 to 4 purple mum stems
- 2 red poppy stems
- 3 goldenrod stems
- 4 white yarrow stems
- flower template
- wired corsage leaves
- 7½" (19cm) diameter ceramic pot
- bolts of red, yellow and blue curling ribbon
- bolt of ⅝" (16mm) rainbow ribbon
- card stock in red, yellow and blue
- red excelsior (CURLY RAFFIA)
- lollipops and hard candy in assorted colors
- dry floral foam brick
- floral anchor
- white waterproof floral tape
- glossy wood-tone spray paint
- hot glue gun
- hole punch

2. birthday favor bag

- small craft paper bag with handle
- lollipop
- flower template
- card stock in red, yellow and blue
- bolts of red, yellow and blue curling ribbon
- red excelsior (CURLY RAFFIA)
- wired corsage leaves
- white floral tape
- hole punch

project 1. **birthday** tree

••• **flower** template

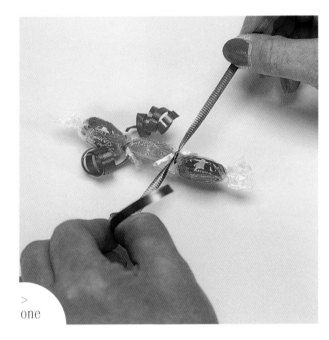

> one

1 create the candy garland

Cut the curling ribbon into 12" (30cm) strips using all three colors. Begin making the garland by tying two pieces of candy together with the curling ribbon in a double knot.

> two

> three

2 curl the ribbon

Curl the ribbon by holding the scissors and ribbon together and pulling along the natural curve of the ribbon. Be sure to hold the ribbon firmly to the scissors with your thumb when pulling.

3 assemble candy garlands

Make 36" (91cm) sections of candy garland by tying the 12" (30cm) sections together. Make as many sections as needed for the branches.

> four

> five

4 make candy flowers

Trace the flower template onto the colored card stock, and cut it out. Use a hole punch to make a hole in the center of the flower, and insert a lollipop.

5 add leaves to flower

Place three corsage leaves under the flower and around the lollipop. Wrap them tightly with floral tape to secure the leaves to the stem.

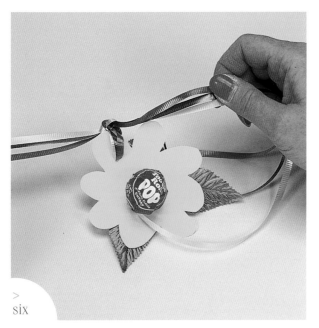

> six

6 create the flower hanger

Cut the lollipop stick to 1" (3cm) or less. Cut three pieces of colored curling ribbon into 30" (76cm) strips. Use a hole punch to make a hole near the center of the flower. Thread all three pieces of ribbon through the hole, and tie near the top of the flower in a double knot. Use the remaining long ends later to tie the flowers to the branches.

> seven

> eight

8 prepare the pot

Hot glue a floral anchor inside the bottom of the pot.

7 prepare tree branches

Using the glossy wood-tone paint, spray the branches to achieve a more polished look.

>
nine

>
ten

9 insert the floral foam

Insert the dry floral foam onto the floral anchor inside the pot.

10 trim the floral foam

Using a knife, trim the floral foam to 1" (3cm) above the rim of the pot. Wedge the scrap pieces of foam into the sides of the pot for better support.

11 insert branches

Insert two to three tree branches into the foam to create a full-looking bush or tree.

>
eleven

> twleve

12 cover foam

Cover the floral foam, the base of the flowerpot and the base of the branches with the red excelsior.

> thirteen

> fourteen

13 insert mums

Cut one purple mum stem to 7" (18cm), and insert into the center of the arrangement. Cut remaining stems into 5" (13cm) sprigs, and insert them randomly throughout the base of the arrangement.

14 insert poppies

Cut two red poppy stems into 5" (13cm) sprigs, and insert them randomly around the base of the arrangement.

> fifteen

> sixteen

15 insert goldenrod

Cut three stems of goldenrod into varying lengths 4" to 7" (10cm to 18cm). Insert them into the arrangement.

16 insert white yarrow

Cut four stems of white yarrow into 5" (13cm) sprigs, and insert them into the arrangement.

> seventeen

17 hang the candy garland

Carefully drape the candy garland onto the branches of the tree.

18 attach candy flowers

Tie the candy flowers onto the branches randomly, and curl the ribbon ends.

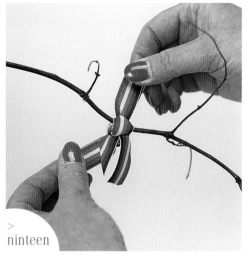

19 tie ribbon bows

Cut the rainbow ribbon into 14" (36cm) pieces, and tie bows randomly onto the branches. Make as many bows as desired.

Designer Tip

Each guest at the birthday party can write messages and birthday wishes on a paper flower and sign the back. Attach these keepsakes to the centerpiece.

birthday favor bag

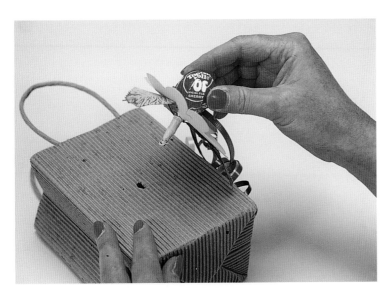

prepare party favor bag

Repeat steps 4 through 6 of the birthday tree (pages 69-70) to create a candy flower for each birthday favor bag. Cut a hole in the upper middle part of the bag, and insert a candy flower with ribbon attached. Curl the ribbon ends with scissors.

Designer Tip

After the bag is filled, tie the handles closed with ribbon. Be sure to curl the ends of the ribbons for a more finished look. Fill the bag with red excelsior, pencils, cookies and other favors .

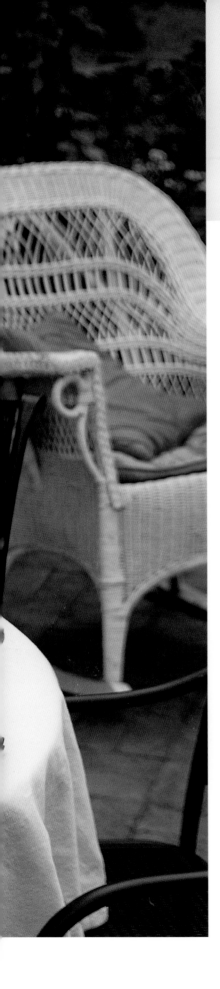

garden party

● **Enjoy good food and warm weather** by choosing an outdoor setting for your party. A romantic garden flower centerpiece arranged in a bird's nest basket and elegant topiary place card holders create a stunning tabletop. Choose linens in pastel colors and lightweight fabrics to set a casual table perfect for relaxing all afternoon. As twilight sets in, scatter short candles anchored in sand and placed in mason jars, antique milk containers and other mismatched glass containers as the perfect extra touch to the table.

PROJECTS

1.
garden party centerpiece
page 78

2.
topiary card holder
page 82

1. garden party centerpiece

- 3 delphinium stems in different colors
- 4 hollyhock stems
- 2 hybrid lily stems
- 3 Queen Anne's lace stems with 3 flower clusters on each
- 4 to 6 English ivy stems
- 6" (15cm) diameter bird's nest basket
- 2 green chenille stems
- dry floral foam brick

2. topiary card holder

- 4 English ivy stems
- 3 delphinium stems in different colors
- 2 corkscrew willow stems
- 4" (10cm) diameter terra-cotta pot
- 3" (8cm) diameter foam ball
- sphagnum moss
- place card
- dry floral foam brick
- floral adhesive
- hot glue gun (OPTIONAL)

project 1.

garden party centerpiece

> one

1 insert floral foam

Cut the floral foam to 5" (13cm), and place it into the bird's nest basket. Cut the remaining pieces of floral foam into smaller pieces and fill in around the foam block in the basket.

> two

2 secure the foam

Twist two chenille stems together to form one long stem. Thread the ends of the extended chenille stem through each side of the basket, wrap the stems around the floral foam and twist to secure.

> four

> three

3 insert delphinium

Cut three stems of delphinium to 22", 24" and 28" (56cm, 61cm and 71cm). Insert the delphinium into the center of the arrangement in a triangle formation.

4 add hollyhock

Cut two 13" (33cm) stems of hollyhock from the top of one stem. Arch and shape the stems to flow downward over the basket edge, and insert them at the base of the delphinium.

5 add lilies

Cut two lily stems to 15" and 17" (38cm and 43cm). Insert the lilies opposite the hollyhocks in the center of the floral foam. Place the tallest lily opposite the tallest delphinium stem. Shape the stems and petals individually.

> five

••• helpful **hint** ••

Flowers naturally grow toward the light, and silk flowers look more natural when they are arranged in this fashion.

> six

> seven

> eight

6 insert Queen Anne's lace

Cut two stems of Queen Anne's lace to 14" and 17" (36cm and 43cm). Insert both stems in the center of the delphinium. Shape and bend the flowers around the other flower stems in the arrangement.

7 add more Queen Anne's lace

Cut the third stem of Queen Anne's lace into three smaller stems from 10" to 12" (25cm to 30cm). Insert them around the base of the arrangement.

8 add more hollyhock

Cut the remaining two stems of hollyhock to 11" (28cm) each. Insert them opposite the other two hollyhock stems, and arch the stems to flow down over the basket.

nine

9 insert English ivy sprigs

Cut staggered lengths of English ivy sprigs from 10" to 18" (25cm to 46cm) long. Insert the ivy sprigs around the base of the arrangement and flowing downward over the basket. Place the longer sprigs in the center of the arrangement near the delphinium. Wrap the ivy around the stems for a more natural look.

Designer Tip

For a more natural look, insert longer ivy sprigs into the basket so that the leaves trail over the edge of the basket and onto the table. Bend the flowers and ivy so that the arangement is loose and informal.

topiary card holder

1 prepare the terra-cotta pot

Cut a small block of dry floral foam to fit inside the terra-cotta pot. Cut an 8" (20cm) stem of thick corkscrew willow, and measure it against the pot and foam ball for the desired height.

2 insert the willow and add moss

Insert the corkscrew willow stem into the center of the floral foam. Add a small amount of floral adhesive or hot glue to the base of the stem to secure it. Put floral adhesive or hot glue on the top of the floral foam, and cover with sphagnum moss.

> one

> two

3 secure the foam ball

Cut a thin corkscrew willow stem to 6" (15cm). Wrap the thin willow stem around the thick topiary stem, and place the foam ball on top of the stems. Press it down until the ball is secure on the willow stems.

4 cover the foam ball

Cut delphinium flowers off the stems, and trim the stems from the back of the flowers so they are flat. Use more than one color of delphinium. Glue the flowers down randomly with floral adhesive or hot glue to completely cover the foam ball.

> three

> four

> five

> six

5 add English ivy

Cut four short sprigs of English ivy, and insert the stems into the floral foam around the base of the topiary. Shape the ivy to trail over the pot.

6 add delphinium at base of topiary

Cut a short stem of delphinium with one flower, and insert it at the base of the topiary. Secure the place card with a dab of glue behind the delphinium.

Designer Tip

For a different look, cover the topiary ball with rose petals or ivy leaves to coordinate with the centerpiece.

romantic dinner for two

● **Enjoy a romantic candlelight dinner** with a table wreath of lush red, pink and white roses. Cluster several pillar candles of various heights in the center of the wreath to softly accent the table. Place an open rose votive candle holder at each place setting. Light scented candles a half hour before the special guest arrives so the room will have a light welcoming fragrance. The combination of colors, lighting, flowers and music will set the mood for love and romance.

PROJECTS

1.
romantic table wreath
page 86

2.
rose votive candle
page 88

1. romantic table wreath

- 3 to 4 pink tiger lily stems
- 12 to 15 medium open deep red rose stems
- 12 to 15 medium open pink rose stems
- 10 to 12 open deep red sweetheart rose spray stems
- 8 to 12 open white sweetheart rose spray stems
- 16" (41cm) diameter foam wreath
- 3 pillar candles in various heights, at least 7" (18cm)
- decorative ribbon
- greening pins
- craft glue
- wire cutters

2. rose votive candle

- 6" (15cm) diameter open deep red rose
- round votive candle holder with candle
- cardboard, at least 5" × 5" (13cm × 13cm)
- hot glue gun

project 1. # romantic table wreath

1 insert tiger lilies

Cut apart the tiger lily stems into six lilies with 1½" (4cm) stems, and insert around the top of the foam wreath.

2 insert roses

Cut all the roses to 1" (3cm) stems, and insert them randomly by color and size to completely cover the wreath. Use craft glue to secure the stem in the foam if it is loose.

> one

> two

> three

3   add rose foliage

Cut the foliage of the unused rose stems into sprigs with 2" (5cm) stems, and insert them randomly throughout the foam wreath to desired fullness. Use greening pins to tuck leaves deeper into the wreath. Tie a ribbon in a square knot around three candles of assorted sizes, and then place them in the center of the wreath. Tie ribbons at least 1" to 2" (3cm to 5cm) from the wick.

● ● ● ● ● ● ● ● ●

Designer Tip

Larger candles give the arrangement more height and drama. Tapers offer a more delicate look.

rose votive candle

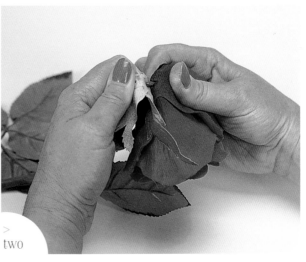

two

1 make votive base

Cut a piece of cardboard into a circle that has a 4½" (11cm) diameter for an open rose with a diameter of 6" (15cm). Cut the leaves off the rose stem, and hot glue the leaves around the outside edge of the round piece of cardboard. Allow the leaves to extend past the edge of the cardboard and overlap for a natural look.

2 prepare rose

Cut the stem completely off the rose leaving it flat on the bottom. Remove the rose petals from the stem.

four

3 remove the flower center

Take each layer of petals off of the center. Remove the center of the rose and discard.

4 prepare the petals

Hold the petal grouping tightly with one hand, and fold an inside petal over the center.

> five

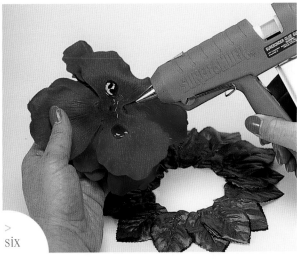

> six

5 staple the petals in place

Staple at the base of the flower petal and off center. Fold one petal over and repeat with the opposite rose petal to form a new flat rose center with the petals.

6 secure rose in place

Hot glue the rose to the cardboard.

Designer Tip

Place a candle and votive holder in the center of the rose. Separate and fluff up the rose petals to make the rose appear more natural.

(LEFT) • **mother's day brunch:**
Multiple dried flower arrangements in terra
cotta pots create a garden-inspired table.

(CENTER) • **christmas at home:**
Victorian Christmas trees and plate wreaths
create a dramatic holiday table full of color.

(RIGHT) • **halloween party:** Let nature
be your guide for this tablesetting featuring
the rich colors of autumn foliage.

● ● ● ● ● ● ● ● ● ● ● ● ●

home for the holidays

Choosing a theme for your holiday decorations makes it easier to harmonize all the rooms in your home. Allow your decorations to be inspired by your personality, heritage, tastes and hobbies.

mother's day brunch
page 92
· ·
halloween party
page 98
· ·
thanksgiving feast
page 106
· ·
christmas at home
page 116

Use the colors of the season as your guide. Choose the bright pastels of spring for Mother's Day, or autumn's lush crimsons, golds and browns for Halloween or Thanksgiving. At Christmastime, red and green are traditional, but you can also achieve great impact with royal blue, purple and metallic tones. In the dining room, coordinate patterned and solid fabrics for the napkins, tablecloth and table runner to transform the space for your celebration. In spring and summer, light cotton and chintz are pleasing fabric choices, and heavier fabrics and textures add warmth during the colder months. Don't forget to bring the outdoors in: show off forced paperwhite or tulip bulbs in spring; bring in nuts, pumpkins and autumn leaves for fall; and take advantage of a variety of greens such as fir, pine, holly and boxwood at Christmas. Nature's bounty takes a lot of the guesswork out of seasonal decorating, guiding you toward inspired holiday entertaining. ●

mother's day brunch

● **Host an unforgettable brunch** for your mother or grandmother to thank her for all that she has done for you. Make her feel special by giving her a day filled with all of her favorite things. Create beautiful dried flower centerpieces that can adorn your table and later become cherished keepsake gifts for your mother. Add coordinated floral napkin rings for a bright, colorful accent on your table. Show her how much she is loved and appreciated by selecting the menu, theme and activities for the day according to your mother's tastes. Celebrate your mother and the beauty of spring with a day filled with beautiful flowers, love and wonderful surprises.

PROJECTS

1.
dried rose centerpiece
page 94

2.
rose napkin ring
page 96

1. dried rose centerpiece

- 6 to 8 dozen dried roses in different colors
- statice stems in three different colors
- feathered eucalyptus
- 5" (13cm) diameter terra-cotta rose pot
- 5" (13cm) diameter foam ball
- terra-cotta markers (OPTIONAL)
- floral lock
- floral adhesive or hot glue gun

2. rose napkin ring

- dried rose
- feathered eucalyptus
- 1¾" (4cm) diameter and ½" (13mm) wide plastic ring
- ⅝" (16mm) grosgrain ribbon, 40" (1m)
- floral adhesive or hot glue gun

project 1. **dried rose** centerpiece

> one

> two

> three

1 decorate terra-cotta pot

Decorate the terra-cotta rose pot with terra-cotta markers (optional).

2 glue foam ball

Spread floral adhesive or hot glue along the inside rim of the terra-cotta pot. Glue a 5" (13cm) diameter foam ball to the pot.

3 add dried roses

Cut the dried roses to 2" (5cm) stems. Begin at the top center of the foam ball, and insert the dried roses of assorted colors. Glue the roses in place with floral lock. When inserting the roses, leave space in between for statice and eucalyptus.

••• helpful **hint** •••

Dried rose stems can be very fragile. Insert a piece of heavy 18-gauge wire into the stem for greater stability. Choose the heaviest of stems to make insertion easier.

> four

> five

4 finish adding roses

Continue to add dried roses of various colors until the foam ball is covered.

5 add statice

Trim the statice to ½" (13mm) stems, not including the length of the flower. Add statice in various colors throughout the arrangement.

> six

6 add feathered eucalyptus

Cut sprigs of eucalyptus leaving at least 1" (3cm) of stem on each leaf. Insert the stems randomly throughout the arrangement to create desired fullness. Trim the leaves to desired length.

••• helpful **hint** •••

Fresh statice and feathered eucalyptus may be substituted for dried. They will dry in the arrangement.

• • • • • • • • • • •

Designer Tip

Dried flowers are very fragile, so store them in a dry and dark place to preserve them. Lightly cover the centerpiece with tissue paper to keep the dust off of it. Spraying a sealant on the centerpiece will help preserve it.

rose napkin ring

> one

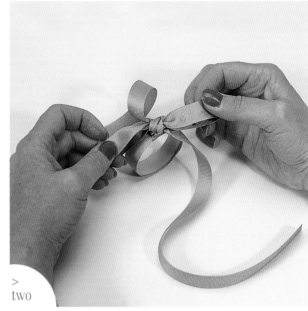

> two

1 glue ribbon

Cut a piece of grosgrain ribbon 10" (25cm) long. Using floral adhesive or hot glue, attach the ribbon around the plastic ring.

2 tie bow

Cut a piece of ribbon 30" (76cm) long. At the seam, tie a bow with a double knot around the ring.

> three

3 trim ribbon

Trim the ribbon ends to the desired length, then fold the ribbon ends in half and cut at an angle.

>
four

••• helpful **hint** •••

Spray sealant on all dried flowers to help
prevent shedding.

4 **insert rose**

Through the knot of the bow, insert a 2" (5cm) dried rose stem,
and add a sprig of feathered eucalyptus.

• • • • • • • • • •

Designer Tip

*Make each napkin ring with
different colors and varieties of roses and
ribbons to make the table come alive
with color and texture.*

halloween party

● **Celebrate the last few days** of Indian summer and the first crisp nights of autumn with a Halloween party. As the trees explode into a myriad of colors, bring those colors into your home with a pumpkin centerpiece brimming over with sunflowers and bittersweet, and with place mats of autumn leaves. Decorate your home with the same crimson, orange, gold and bronze colors that are seen in nature. Mums, Indian corn, gourds in assorted shapes and colors and pumpkins capture the spirit of the fall harvest. Let the aromas of pumpkin pie, apples and cinnamon fill your home to create a cozy evening with friends and family.

PROJECTS

1.

pumpkin centerpiece
page 100

2.

autumn leaves place mat
page 105

1. pumpkin centerpiece

- 2 winterberry stems
- 6 to 10 purple berry cluster stems
- autumn leaf bush
- 2 bittersweet bushes
- sunflower bush
- foam pumpkin
- dry floral foam brick
- 2 floral anchors
- 12" (30cm) floral pick
- floral adhesive or hot glue gun

2. autumn leaves place mat

- one bunch of dried autumn leaves
- 12" × 18" (30cm × 46cm) cardboard
- 12" × 18" (30cm × 46cm) mesh batting
- moss green spray paint
- floral adhesive or hot glue gun

project 1. # **pumpkin** centerpiece

>
one

1 carve pumpkin

Carve a 4" (10cm) diameter opening in the top of the pumpkin.

>
two

2 secure floral anchors

Glue two floral anchors with floral adhesive or hot glue to the bottom of the inside of the pumpkin. Allow to dry for five minutes.

> three

> four

3 insert floral foam

Insert the block of floral foam inside the pumpkin and onto the floral anchors. Cut the top of the foam to leave 1" (3cm) of floral foam above the pumpkin opening.

4 add autumn leaves

Cut the leaf bush into 10" (25cm) stems, and insert them randomly around the arrangement. Bend the stems and allow them to trail along the bottom of the arrangement for a more natural look.

> five

> six

5 insert autumn leaf sprigs

Randomly insert the remaining smaller 5" to 6" (13cm to 15cm) sprigs of autumn leaves throughout the centerpiece.

6 add bittersweet

Cut the two bittersweet bushes into 8" (20cm) stems. Insert them randomly throughout the centerpiece.

>
seven

>
eight

7 add winterberry

Insert one 18" (46cm) stem of winterberry in the center of the foam.

8 fill in with smaller winterberry

From the second stem of winterberry, cut 8" (20cm) branches of winterberry clusters. Insert these stems throughout the centerpiece.

9 cut sunflower bush

Cut the stems from the sunflower bush, keeping the longest sunflower stem approximately 15" (38cm). Insert the 15" (38cm) stem into the center of the foam.

>
nine

> ten

> eleven

> twelve

10 fill in with sunflowers

Insert the remaining sunflowers randomly throughout the arrangement.

11 trim the purple berry stems

Trim the berry sprigs from the stems, leaving two berry sprigs attached to one of the thicker main stems. Insert the main stem with sprigs off center into the top of the foam.

12 insert berry sprigs

Fill in the arrangement with 5" (13cm) purple berry sprigs.

13 attach pumpkin lid

Insert the pointed edge of a 12"
(30cm) floral pick into the side of the
pumpkin lid, then insert it off center
into the foam.

> thirteen

Designer Tip

*Cut leftover leaves from the branches, and
place them randomly around the table for
decoration. Cut 8" (20cm) bittersweet sprigs,
and wrap them around the napkins
as napkin rings.*

autumn leaves place mat

> one

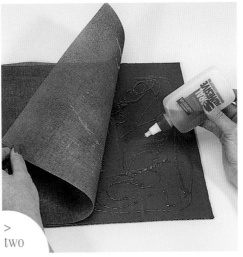

> two

1 prepare cardboard

Spray the piece peice of cardboard with moss green spray paint. Allow it to dry.

2 prepare and attach batting

Spray a the batting with moss green spray paint. Allow it to dry. Using floral adhesive or a hot glue gun, attach the batting to the cardboard. Allow it to dry.

> three

3 secure autumn leaves

Apply floral adhesive or hot glue to the batting and to the back of the autumn leaves. Lay the leaves on the mat in all directions and overlap them. Be sure to let leaves hang over the cardboard edge slightly for a more natural look.

Designer Tip

Use sheets of wax paper between the place mats when you store them to prevent the leaves from sticking together.

thanksgiving feast

● **Enjoy a cozy and inviting Thanksgiving** meal with family and friends at a table decorated with a warm jewel-tone centerpiece of lush autumn florals and fruit. Accent a serving platter with a grapevine ivy garland perfect for showing off a beautiful turkey or other traditional dish. Create a festive table by decorating with dried maple leaves, miniature pumpkins or gourds, acorns and other nuts. Celebrate the harvest season in style, and remember all that you have to be thankful for this year.

PROJECTS

1.
thanksgiving centerpiece
page 108

2.
serving platter ivy garland
page 115

1. thanksgiving centerpiece

- 1 eucalyptus stem
- 3 cosmos stems with 3 flowers and 1 bud on each (I USED 2 YELLOW AND 1 LIGHT BROWN COSMOS.)
- 4 large open-rose stems (I USED 2 DEEP PURPLE AND 2 BURGUNDY ROSES.)
- 3 open-rose spray stems
- 5 mountain ash with berries stems
- 3 frosted wild berry stems
- 1 ranunculus stem
- 1 black-eyed Susan stem
- 1 winterberry stem
- 2 pepper berry bushes
- 1 grapevine foliage bush
- grapevine ivy garland

- 6 bunches of grapes (2 PURPLE, 4 GREEN)
- 11" × 18" (28cm × 46cm) basket
- 3 pheasant feathers, 17" (43cm), 5 pheasant feathers, 10" to 12" (25cm to 30cm)
- dry floral foam brick
- 6 to 10 floral picks with wire
- 5 green chenille stems

2. serving platter ivy garland

- 3 cosmos stems
- grapevine ivy garland
- paddle wire

project 1.

thanksgiving centerpiece

>
one

>
two

1 attach the foam to the basket

Twist the ends of three chenille stems together to make one long chenille stem, and twist two chenille stems together to make a second long chenille stem. Wrap the shorter of the combined chenille stems around the width of the dry foam, and wrap the longer one around the length of the dry foam. Insert the ends into the bottom of the basket.

2 secure the foam

To secure the floral foam, twist the stems together under the basket like a package. Don't pull the chenille stems too tightly or they will slice through the floral foam.

••• helpful **hint** •••

Cover the chenille stems at the bottom of the basket with masking tape to protect the table finish.

> three

3 insert eucalyptus

Cut the stem of eucalyptus into two sprigs, 18" (46cm) and 16" (41cm). Insert one sprig at an angle to the left of center and the other at an angle to the right of center.

> four

> five

4 add cosmos

Cut the three stems of cosmos into three sprigs, for a total of nine. For each stem, cut one sprig to 12" (30cm) with flower and bud, one sprig to 8" to 10" (20cm to 25cm) and the last sprig remaining with a flower to 6" to 8" (15cm to 20cm). Insert the two longest sprigs close to the center and the shorter one farther out. Insert two long sprigs on either end of the arrangement. Insert the shorter sprigs randomly throughout.

5 add open roses

Cut two deep purple open roses and two burgundy open roses to have 7" (18cm) stems from the base of the flower head. If there are thorns, trim them off because they will break the foam. Insert the burgundy roses on opposite sides. Insert the deep purple roses in opposite corners of the burgundy roses.

> six

> seven

6 insert pepper berry bushes

Insert the pepper berry bushes opposite each other in the center of the arrangement. Spread out the branches.

7 add open-rose sprays

Cut three open-rose sprays into 5" to 8" (13cm to 20cm) sprigs, and insert them randomly throughout the arrangement.

8 add mountain ash with berries

Using five stems of mountain ash, cut two sprigs from each stem to 13" (33cm) and 11" (28cm). Cut the remaining sprigs from each stem to 7" (18cm) each. Insert the tall sprigs in the center of the arrangement, and randomly insert the shorter sprigs throughout. Randomly insert any remaining foliage from the stems in the centerpiece as well.

> eight

> nine

9 insert frosted wild berries

Cut one stem of frosted wild berries to 16" (41cm), and insert it in the center. Trim the branches off the other two stems to 7" to 11" (18cm to 28cm), and add randomly throughout the arrangement.

> ten

10 add ranunculus

Cut three 7" to 11" (18cm to 28cm) sprigs from one ranunculus stem. Insert two sprigs on one side of the basket and one on the other.

> eleven

11 add black-eyed Susans

Cut one black-eyed Susan stem into three sprigs measuring 7" to 13" (18cm to 33cm) each. Randomly insert them into the basket so they are visually balanced.

> twelve

12 attach grape bunches to floral picks

Attach each bunch of grapes to a floral pick by twisting the wire around the end of the grape bunch.

>
thirteen

13 insert grape bunches

Insert the grape bunches into the arrangement around the base. Tuck them in deep, and allow the grapes to flow over the edge of the basket.

>
fourteen

14 add winterberry

Cut one winterberry stem into four 7" (18cm) sprigs. Insert two sprigs on each side of the basket.

>
sixteen

16 add grapevine foliage

Cut grapevine stems from the bush, and randomly insert them into any open spaces in the arrangement.

>
fifteen

15 insert pheasant feathers

Insert three 17" (43cm) feathers into the center of the arrangement. Insert five 10" to 12" (25cm to 30cm) feathers throughout the centerpiece.

Designer Tip

Cover any imperfections in the basket with foliage or grapes by strategically placing stems.

serving platter ivy garland

> one

> two

**1 measure
grapevine garland**

Place the grapevine garland around the base of your platter, and trim to size. Measure the garland so that it fits snugly under the lip of the platter for better presentation.

2 Add cosmos

Cut nine 7" (18cm) sprigs from three stems of cosmos, and secure the stems together by wrapping them with paddle wire. Insert them into the garland. For a fuller appearance, add more cosmos stems. Double-wrap the paddle wire for extra hold.

3 secure ends of garland

Attach the ends of the garland together with paddle wire.

> three

Designer Tip

*Place the garland under the lip of
the platter, and bend the flowers
to the position desired.*

christmas at home

● **Enjoy a festive holiday dinner party** with beautiful Victorian Christmas tree centerpieces and dramatic plate wreaths. Make your dining table the focal point by using luxurious fabrics, fine silverware and glittering china. Hang fir branches, ivy, mistletoe and holly on the mantel with Christmas stockings to create a winter wonderland. Add small white candles or holiday lights around your home to enhance the magical feeling of the season. Celebrate with friends and family using new and old traditions to create a memorable holiday.

PROJECTS

1.
christmas tree centerpiece
page 118

2.
winterberry plate wreath
page 123

materials:

1. christmas tree centerpiece

- 1 to 2 dozen winterberry stems
- 8 to 10 dozen dried red rose buds (SOLD IN BAGS)
- 2 to 3 dozen dried white roses
- 5 to 6 boxwood garlands, 3 yards (3m) each
- 24" (61cm) tall foam cone
- 42 to 52 cinnamon sticks, 3" (8cm) each
- 6 yards (5m) of ¼" (6mm) red satin picot ribbon
- 20 yards (18m) of ⅜" (10mm) gold metallic ribbon
- greening pins
- moss green spray paint
- floral adhesive or hot glue gun
- sewing needle
- elastic thread

2. winterberry plate wreath

- 1 to 2 dozen winterberry stems
- 5 to 6 boxwood garlands, 3 yards (3m) each
- 14" (36cm) diameter green foam wreath
- 8 yards (8m) of ½" (13mm) red satin picot ribbon
- greening pins

project 1.

christmas tree centerpiece

>
one

1 paint tree

Using moss green spray, paint the foam cone.

>
two

2 secure boxwood garland

Secure the end of the first boxwood garland to the top of the foam cone with a greening pin.

••• helpful **hint** •••

The tree will appear fuller the closer together and tighter you wrap the garland around the foam cone.

> three

> four

> five

3 wrap the boxwood garlands

Begin to tightly wrap the boxwood garland around the foam cone, and secure it by inserting the greening pins into the garland and the foam along the way. Continue to add garlands until the entire cone is covered. Secure the ends of the garlands with greening pins.

4 create rosebud garland

Thread a needle with elastic thread, and string dried red rose buds to make a garland. Knot the thread on either end of the garland to secure the roses. Thread at least eight dozen dried roses on the garland.

5 wrap the rose garland

Wrap the rose garland from top to bottom around the tree using greening pins to secure it to the foam.

>
six

>
seven

6 make ribbon garland

Take approximately 6 yards of ¼" (6mm) red satin picot ribbon, and create a garland by making a shoestring bow every
10" to 12" (25cm to 30cm) along the ribbon.

7 wrap the ribbon garland

Wrap the ribbon garland around the cone using the greening pins to secure the garland.

8 make cinnamon ornament

Cut a 16" (41cm) length of gold metallic ribbon. Make an X
with two cinnamon sticks, and wrap a ribbon around the
center. Crisscross the ribbon and wrap it the opposite way to
hold the sticks securely together in an X.

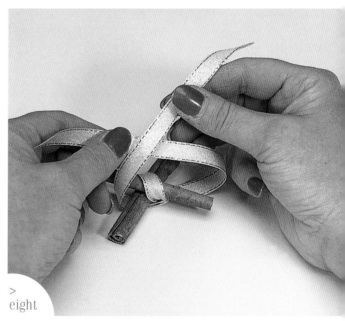

>
eight

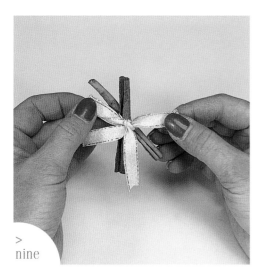

> nine

> ten

9 make a bow

Tie the ends of the ribbon into a bow.

10 attach ribbon hanger

Cut a 12" (30cm) length of gold metallic ribbon, and tie it onto the cinnamon ornament. Then tie the ends of the ribbon in a knot, leaving a loop for hanging.

> eleven

11 attach the ornament

Attach the ornament to the cone with a greening pin. Repeat steps 8 through 10 to make twenty to twenty-five additional ornaments as desired, and place them randomly around the tree.

12 prepare white roses

Cut the desired number of white rose stems to 2" (5cm). Insert the white rose stems randomly around the cone into the foam. Use floral adhesive or a hot glue gun to secure the stems.

13 add winterberry stems

Cut sprigs of winterberry to 2" (5cm) stems, and insert them randomly around the cone as desired.

> twelve

> thirteen

● ● ● ● ◦ ◦ ● ● ● ●

Designer Tip

Place plastic bags over each Christmas tree in order to preserve the fragile flowers. Store the centerpieces in a dry and dark place because the dried flowers can fade and deteriorate in humidity and sunlight.

winterberry plate wreath

> one

> two

2 **fill in the center of the wreath**

Fill in the center of the wreath with small sprigs of boxwood.

1 **cover the wreath**

Wrap the foam wreath completely with boxwood garlands.

Secure the garlands with greening pins.

> three

3 **cut and wrap the ribbon**

Cut two 4-yard (4m) lengths of ½"
(13mm) red satin picot ribbon. Use
the first ribbon to wrap the wreath,
and secure with greening pins.

> four

> five

4 wrap the second ribbon

Wrap and crisscross the second ribbon around the wreath, and secure with greening pins.

5 add winterberry sprigs

Cut sprigs of winterberry from the stems, and insert them randomly around the wreath. Fill in to desired fullness.

• • • • • • • • • •

Designer Tip

If you want a smaller wreath with less fullness, use a thinner foam base. You can also hang the wreath on a door or wall and display it throughout the holiday season.

W.J. Cowee, Inc.
28 Taylor Ave.
P.O. Box 248
Berlin, NY 12022
Phone: (518) 658-2233
Fax: (518) 658-2244
www.cowee.com

• Floral picks and general floral supplies

Design Master Color Tool, Inc.
P.O. Box 601
Boulder, CO 80306
Phone: (303) 443-5214
Fax: (303) 443-5217
www.dmcolor.com

• Floral scents, floral color sprays, paints and tints

Floracraft
1 Longfellow Place
P.O. Box 400
Ludington, MI 49431
Phone: (231) 845-0240
www.floracraft.com

• Floral sheet foam and general floral supplies

Mariemont Florist, Inc.
7257 Wooster Pike
Cincinnati, OH 45227
Phone: (800) 437-3567
Fax: (513) 271-7484
www.mariemontflorist.com

• Author contact, general information and assistance

Oasis Floral Products
P.O. Box 118
Kent, OH 44240
Phone: (800) 321-8286
Fax: (800) 447-0813
www.smithersoasis.com

• Floral foam products

In addition to the mail-order and online resources
listed here, check your local craft and floral supply
shops for general floral tools and supplies.
Purchase fine silk and dried flowers from local craft
stores or directly from your florist.

a

Adhesive, 14
Air-drying flowers and plants, 17
Amaranthus, 34, 49
Anchor, 14
Autumn leaves, 101
Autumn leaves place mats, 105

b

Birthday favor bag, 75
Birthday Surprise, 66-75
Birthday tree centerpiece, 68-74
Bittersweet, 101
Black-eyed susans, 112
Boxwood, 118-119
Bridesmaid Tea Party, 58-65

c

Candle adapter, 14
Candleholders
    floral, 52-55
    river cane candle trivet, 45
    votive candle holder, 25, 88-89
Candles, 12
    staggering, 24
Card holders
    topiary, 82-83
Centerpieces
    birthday tree, 68-74
    Christmas tree, 118-122
    dried rose, 94-95
    garden party, 78-81
    magnolia, 22-24
    orchid, 38-44
    pumpkin, 100-104
    romantic table wreath, 86-87
    rose, 48-51
    safari, 30-34
    sweetheart rose topiary, 60-63
    Thanksgiving, 108-114
Chenille stem, 14
Christmas at Home, 116-122
Christmas tree centerpiece, 118-122
Cinnamon, 120
Corkscrew willow, 42, 82
Cosmos, 61, 109, 115

d

Dark green ivy, 62
Decorative details, 11
Delphinium, 50, 54, 79, 83
Dinner Parties, 18-55
    Night in the Far East, A, 20-27
    South Seas Paradise, 37-45
    White Elegance, 46-55
    Into the Wild, 28-35
Dried flowers and plants, 17
Dried rose centerpiece, 94-95

e

English ivy, 50, 54, 81, 83
Eucalyptus, 95, 109

f

Favor boxes and bags
    birthday favor bag, 75
    potpourri favor box, 64-65
Floral adhesive, 14
Floral anchor, 14
Floral candleholders, 52-55
Floral foam, 14
Floral pick, 14
Floral scent, 14
Floral spray paint, 14
Floral tape, 14
Flowers and plants
    air-drying, 17
    amaranthus, 34, 49
    autumn leaves, 101
    bittersweet, 101
    Black-eyed susans, 112
    boxwood, 118-119
    cinnamon, 120
    corkscrew willow, 42, 82
    cosmos, 61, 109, 115
    dark green ivy, 62
    delphinium, 50, 54, 79, 83
    dried, 17
    English ivy, 50, 54, 81, 83
    eucalyptus, 95, 109
    freeze-drying, 17
    galax leaves, 25
    goldenrod, 73
    grape bunches, 112-113
    grapevine, 114-115
    hollyhock, 79-80
    iris grass, 25
    lilies, 79
    lisianthus, 50
    magnolias, 22-24, 61
    mountain ash, 110
    mums, 72
    orchids, 38-44
    pepper berries, 110
    poppies, 49, 72
    protea, 33
    purple berries, 103
    Queen Anne's lace, 80
    ranunculus, 111
    river cane, 38-45
    roses, 48-51, 86-87, 94-97, 109-110, 119, 122
    silica gel, 17
    silk flowers, 16
    sphagnum moss, 22, 33, 82
    statice, 95
    sunflowers, 102
    sweetheart roses, 61
    thistle, 33
    tiger lilies, 86
    variegated ivy, 62
    white yarrow, 73
    wild berries, 61, 111
    winterberries, 113, 122
    winterberry, 102
Foam, 14
Freeze-drying flowers and plants, 17

g

Galax leaf place mats, 35
Garden Party, 76-83
Garden party centerpiece, 78-81
Goldenrod, 73
Grape bunches, 112-113
Grapevine, 114-115
Greening pin, 14

h

Halloween Party, 98-105
Holidays, 90-124

index

Christmas at Home, 116-122
Halloween Party, 98-105
Mother's Day Brunch, 92-97
Thanksgiving Feast, 106-115
Hollyhock, 79-80
Hot glue gun, 14

i-l

Into the Wild, 28-35
Introduction, 9-13
Iris grass, 25
Ivy garland serving platter, 115
Lighting, 12
Lilies, 79
Lisianthus, 50

m

Magnolia centerpiece, 22-24
Magnolias, 61
Mood, creating, 12-13
Mother's Day Brunch, 92-97
Mountain ash, 110
Mums, 72

n-o

Napkin rings
  galax leaves, 35
  rose, 96-97
Night in the Far East, A, 20-27
Orchid centerpiece, 38-44
Outdoors, entertaining, 13

p

Paddle wire, 14
Pebble place mat, 26-27
Pepper berries, 110
Pheasant feathers, 114
Pick, 14
Place mats
  autumn leaves, 105
  galax leaf, 35
  multiple, 27
  pebble place mat, 26-27
Plant stake, 15

Plants. see Flowers and plants
Plate wreath, winterberry, 123-124
Poppies, 49, 72
Potpourri favor box, 64-65
Protea, 33
Pumpkin centerpiece, 100-104
Purple berries, 103

q-r

Queen Anne's lace, 80
Ranunculus, 111
Resources, 125
River cane candle trivet, 45
Romantic Dinner for Two, 84-89
Romantic table wreath centerpiece, 86-87
Rose centerpiece, 48-51
Roses, 86-87, 94-97, 109-110, 119, 122

s

Safari centerpiece, 30-34
Scent, 14
Sealer, 15
Serving platter
  ivy garland, 115
Silica gel, flowers and plants, 17
Silk flowers, 16
South Seas Paradise, 37-45
Special Occasions, 56-89
  Birthday Surprise, 66-75
  Bridesmaid Tea Party, 58-65
  Garden Party, 76-83
  Romantic Dinner for Two, 84-89
Sphagnum moss, 22, 33, 82
Spray paint, 14
Statice, 95
Sunflowers, 102
Supplies
  candle adapter, 14
  chenille stem, 14
  floral adhesive, 14
  floral anchor, 14
  floral foam, 14
  floral pick, 14
  floral scent, 14
  floral spray paint, 14
  floral tape, 14

  greening pin, 14
  hot glue gun, 14
  paddle wire, 14
  plant stake, 15
  sealer, 15
  wire cutter, 15
Sweetheart roses, 61

t

Tape, 14
Thanksgiving centerpiece, 108-114
Thanksgiving Feast, 106-115
Theme, creating, 10
Thistle, 33
Tiger lilies, 86
Tools. see Supplies
Topiary card holder, 82-83

v-w

Variegated ivy, 62
Votive candle holder, 25, 88-89
White Elegance, 46-55
White yarrow, 73
Wild berries, 61, 111
Winterberries, 102, 113, 122
Winterberry plate wreath, 123-124
Wire cutter, 15

Create gorgeous gifts and decorations with silk and dried flowers!

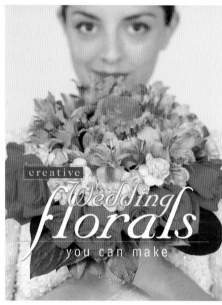

- Capture the essence of the seasons with these simple, stunning floral arrangements. With a few basic techniques, a handful of materials, and a little creativity, you can make eye-pleasing accents for every room in your home. You'll find all the flower arranging advice you need inside, along with 15 projects using silk flowers, greenery, leaves, pinecones, gourds and more.

ISBN 1-58180-108-4, paperback, 96 pages, #31810-K

- Whether you're the bride-to-be, a member of the wedding party, or a close friend, this book can show you how to create gorgeous floral arrangements for priceless wedding memories. You'll find guidelines for crafting 20 step-by-step projects, from the bride's bouquet and boutonnieres to pew decorations and wedding cake toppers.

ISBN 1-55870-560-0, paperback, 128 pages, #70488-K

- Here are 20 beautiful wreath projects, perfect for brightening up a doorway or celebrating a special time of year. You'll find a range of sizes and styles, utilizing a variety of creative materials, including dried herbs, sea shells, cinnamon sticks, silk flowers, Autumn leaves, Christmas candy and more. Clear, step-by-step instructions ensure beautiful, long lasting results every time!

ISBN 1-58180-239-0, paperback, 144 pages, #32015-K

These books and other fine **North Light** craft titles are available from your local art & craft retailer, bookstore, online supplier or by calling **1-800-289-0963**.